Heinrich Heine, Rennell Rodd

The Unknown Madonna and other Poems

Heinrich Heine, Rennell Rodd

The Unknown Madonna and other Poems

ISBN/EAN: 9783744712309

Printed in Europe, USA, Canada, Australia, Japan

Cover: Foto ©Thomas Meinert / pixelio.de

More available books at **www.hansebooks.com**

AVE MARIA

THE

UNKNOWN MADONNA

AND OTHER POEMS

I.—POEMS IN MANY LANDS. SECOND SERIES

II.—IN EXCELSIS

III.—TRANSLATIONS FROM HEINE

BY

RENNELL RODD

AUTHOR OF "POEMS IN MANY LANDS" AND "FEDA"

WITH A FRONTISPIECE BY W. B. RICHMOND, A.R.A.

LONDON

DAVID STOTT, 370, OXFORD STREET, W.

MDCCCLXXXVIII.

TO MY CHIEF

SIR EDWARD MALET

I DEDICATE THESE POEMS.

BERLIN, 1888.

I have to acknowledge the courtesy of Messrs. SCRIBNER and Messrs. MACMILLAN for permission to reprint the poems on pages 9 and 17.

R. R.

CONTENTS.

———+———

THE UNKNOWN MADONNA.

I KNOW that picture's meaning,— the unknown,
Called School of Umbria ; it stands alone ;
Those prayerful fingers never worked to fame,—
A master's hand, though silence keeps his name.
But for the meaning, gaze awhile and plain
The thought he worked in warms to life again :
Love made those features living, such a face
Smiled once,—on whom ?   Say in a lofty place
He could not climb to,—in those eyes' blue deeps
The reverence of unreached ideals keeps
The human memory, not a face of dreams,
And coldly beautiful, but one that seems
Caught in the likeness that a lover's eyes
Devoutly worshipped to idealize ;
And since creation is akin to prayer
He made that face God's Mother, and set her there
Among the lilies by the hill-side town.

B

And then the child, a flower-face to crown
The human love-dream, little hands entwined
Round one surrendered finger, to my mind
Just such close watching, tenderness expressed
As those who miss it learn to look for best.
Perugian, say we,—look, the lilies lean
Against the mountain, dips the vale between,
Yonder's Assisi on the nearer ridge,
And that's the gorge that hides the giant bridge
Joining Spoleto, and beyond, away
Hill-crests like waves in purple to midday.
That was his thought, to make his art her shrine,
And lift her human up to the divine;
So smiles Madonna, so evermore sits she
Against the Umbrian blue mountain sea.

Why do I think so?   Why, because if I
Could paint just one such picture ere I die,
Make one thought everlasting, I would choose
His theme, the Mother and the Child, and use
A face as sweet as this was; in the Child
Reflect its beauty, only undefiled
Of pain and sorrow and knowledge, and would set

Both in a garden that is lilied yet
With beds her own hands tended, and enclose
All in a girdle of the hills she chose
Of earth's fair homes to dwell in, keeping so
The tender fragrance of dead years ago.

  I would not change these few square feet for halls
Of Ghirlandajo, for the magic walls
Of this your Cambio,—I would rather keep
My silent record of his nameless sleep,
Dream back his story through the long blank years—
Believe those lilies once were dewed with tears.

PERUGIA.

DANTE'S GRAVE.

THERE is an awe, I know not whence or why,
About the graves where sleep the mighty dead,
There is an instinct guides our feet to track
The path they travelled ; these have led me here.
This is Ravenna, in the midnight hour
Of windless silence, the blank windows stare
Like eyes that time has blinded through the night
From ruins and half-ruins, and my step
Startles the haunted echoes.   It is here !
Vast in the shadows, San Francesco looms
Against the quick Italian stars, one lamp
Confirms the cloister's gloom, a willow tree
Droops to a grill of iron, and within
Dark cypress clusters : this is Dante's grave !

　Far from the Tuscan mountains and the vale
Loved with a patriot's passion, here he died,
Unpardoned, unforgiving, unsubdued.

Oh great sad constant soul that stood for God
In a wild world of discord, though you climbed
Steep stairs of alien palaces, and knew
How salt the bread of exiles, failing friends
And misconceived ideals,—where are they
Who sat in the high places ! Time has made
Thy scorn their only monument, and dimmed
Each lesser lustre round thy lonely star !
Not all unrecompensed on earth ! For thine
The faith which ventures the ideal love,
The crown which envy cannot clutch, the faith
Which feels how vainly venomed arrows strike
The flawless armour of a pure intent ;
And the ideal love leaned down from heaven
To win thee from false idols, and reveal
Tier after tier to the last murky deep
The doom that passes pardon, urged thee mount
Hard ridge by ridge the penitential hill,
Through the terrestrial Eden, to attain
The mysteries of the rose of Paradise.

Oh stern of tenure to thy purpose high !
Oh, hard to love, compelling to revere !

For all the wanderings of thy exile feet
Be earth's remorse our reverence and our hope !

For hope is child of wisdom, and despair
The bastard of half-knowledge.   O'er this grave
The soft quick stars have climbed and set again,
The rose he loved has flushed the morning east,
The snows along the back of Apennine
Have blanched and thawed through five long hundred
          years,
And man has marched not vainly the steep road
Proclaimed by priests and poets. Soon, aye now,
We almost need thy grisly hell no more !
We have outgrown the visionary doom
That waits on sin's hereafter, Love not Fear
Urges our progress up the purging hill,
Where man must answer for his fellow man :
And new ideals have set heaven so high
We miss thy clearer vision, nor complain !
Our years are dim with struggle, as were thine,
But lit with gleams of promise, where at times
The herald watchers on the heights discern
Far peaks of that first Eden which is spread
Nearest the confines of the light of God.

DANTE'S GRAVE.

Ah, lonely city of the marshy mead,
Left lonelier by the ever-ebbing sea,
Keep thou thy guest and guard his sacred sleep :
The poet's refuge, be the poet's grave !
Well rests he here, dead reed of deathless song,
Where silence feeds on echoes of mute names,
Shrouded in memories, famous and forlorn !

RAVENNA.

MARCH.

Such blue of sky, so palely fair,
Such glow of earth, such lucid air!
Such purple on the mountain lines,
Such deep new verdure in the pines!
The live light strikes the broken towers,
The crocus bulbs burst into flowers,
The sap strikes up the black vine stock,
And the lizard wakes in the splintered rock,
The wheat's young green peeps through the sod,
And the heart is touched with a thought of God;
The very silence seems to sing,
It must be spring, it must be spring!

OCTOBER.

A FITFUL wind about the eaves,
    That sways the creaking door;
The shadows of the falling leaves
    Flit past me on the floor.

The autumn skies are clear above,
    But silent is their song;
Oh, spirit of the changeless love,
    Keep back my autumn long!

In vain with gold the forest weaves
    Its sylvan greenness o'er;
The shadows of the falling leaves
    Flit past me on the floor.

It means the world is growing old,
    It means no birds to sing;
Oh, not for all the autumn's gold
    Would I forego my spring!

THE GONDOLA.

WE do not speak but hearken
 To softly plashing oars,
We watch the wide way darken
 Between the lighted shores,
While sable-hulled and silver-prowed
 Slide past the phantom boats,
And near and far, now low, now loud
 A drifting music floats :
They only have one song to sing,
The song of youth and love and spring.

And where St. George's Island
 Looms o'er the dark lagoon,
Slow through the rifts in sky-land
 Sails up the golden moon ;
Now I can see your shadowy hair,
 And read your dreaming eyes,
So sweet, almost the old despair,
 The dirge of memory dies ;
Oh, only teach me to forget,
And I may learn to love you yet !

THE WANDERER'S SONG.

Day is dead, and blent in shadow
  Lies the ridge that crowns his tomb,
Mists are rising from the meadow,
  And the woods are massed in gloom.
Homeward bells of lowing cattle
  Sound along the village street,
And the gossips' shrilling prattle,
  And the children's running feet.

Cool the fountain water splashes,
  And the lights show one by one,
While the first star faintly flashes
  In the gold wake of the sun.
Silent groups return from reaping
  With a reverence past the shrine—
Hold you God in His good keeping,
  Give you lighter hearts than mine !

Out beyond the hills that bound you
   Deeds are done and thoughts are thought—
Such a battle rages round you,
   But it vexes you in naught :
Evening air a-scent with clover,
   And the peat-smoke softly curled
Up the dark hill-side and over—
   This is all your little world !

Have ye other lives to travel,
   Quiet dwellers in the trees,
Deeper problems to unravel
   Than the darkest drift of these ?
Loftier aims in other ages,
   Wider orbits, keener fears?
Rest you now ! for labour's wage is
   Dreamless sleep and quick-dried tears.

Here men change not, men desire not,
   Here men wander not away ;
Here they fail not who aspire not,
   Here are still content to pray,

Such a rest from all the riot!
  Fairest valley that thou art,
This contagion of thy quiet
  Spreads its twillight on my heart.

Now the mountains lie in trances,
  All the forests sway in dreams,
And the moon with silver lances
  Strikes the ever-waking streams :
Waking stream, we race together,
  Rush and swirl and even flow,
Breasting crags or skirting heather
  To a sea we neither know.

Your swift eddies envy surely,
  As they near the rocky leap,
Yonder lake that lies so purely
  Hardly rippled in its sleep ;
So, half-envious, I too linger,
  Pace the village to and fro,
While yon peak gleams like a finger
  Pointing skyward through the snow ;

Then away—and no returning!
  Whirls the eddy down the gorge,
Where, night through, the fires are burning,
  And the sparks fly from the forge.
On, till these blue stars are setting,
  And the dawn unrobes the sky!
Such an Eden of forgetting
  I would ask for when I die!

TYROL.

AVE MARIA.

Ave Maria ! Day declines,
  Grows the peace of the evening star,
Shadows rise on the mountain lines,—
  Wide the heaven and God so far !
How should He stoop to the human sin !
Mother and human take me in !
  Thou hast suffered, and thou canst see,
    Ave Maria, Ave Marie !

Ave Maria ! At end of day
  Rings thy peal on the evening air,
Calls the world to its homeward way,
  Stays the heart in a pause of prayer :
Ave Maria, by storm or star,
The thought of the wanderer turns from far
  To the shrine of his haven,—Light of the Sea !
    Ave Maria, Ave Marie !

Ave Maria ! Years roll by,
 Thy dominion shall endure,
All who make for the hard and high,
 All the chivalrous brave and pure,
Kneel in heart at an inward shrine,
Built for a woman, and therefore thine,
 For we lift our love to the light of thee,
  Ave Maria, Ave Marie !

CHRISTMAS EVE.

A GERMAN STUDY.

LITTLE mother, why must you go!
  The children play by the white bed-side,
  The world is merry for Christmas-tide,
What would you do in the falling snow!

They sleep by now in the ember-glow,
  Hushed to dream in a child's delight,
  For wonders happen on Christmas night:
Little mother, why must you go!

The still flakes fall and the night grows late,
  Oh slender figure and small wet feet,
  Where do you haste through the lamplit street,
And out and away by the fortress gate?

It's drear and chill where the dear lie dead!
  Yet light enough with the snow to see:
  But what would you do with that Christmas tree,
At the tiny mound that is baby's bed?

C

A Christmas tree, with its tinsel gold !—
   Oh, how should I not have a thought for thee
   When the children sleep in their dream of glee,
Poor little grave but a twelvemonth old !

Little mother, your heart is brave,
   You kiss the cross in the drifted snow,
   Kneel for a moment, rise and go,
And leave your tree by the tiny grave.

While the living slept by the warm fireside,
   And the snows fell white on your Christmas toy,
   I think that its angel wept for joy,
Because you remembered the one that died.

TOURGUÉNEFF.

OH watcher of the night, what cheer to see?
　A fruitless fret and fume of uncontent,
A world of shadows wandering aimlessly,
　A weary purpose and a heart long spent ;

　A hand of iron reaching everywhere,
　　And over-clouded skies where no stars shine,
A flock without a shepherd, and despair
　Gazing across the darkness for a sign ;

A crowd of preachers without faith or creed,
　And here and there, to break the monotone,
The passing wonder of a golden deed—
　A sacrifice, unrecompensed, unknown.

And is that all?　Not quite ; beside the bier
　Where youth lies self-devoted, far and faint
Above the world's scorn crying " fool," I hear
　Another voice that seems to answer " saint."

VENICE.

SAN SERVOLO.

THE isles are purpled in the haze,
We leave the dark canals and pass
    To open water ways,
The noon sky burns like burnished brass,
    The yellow waters glare :
The Euganéan mountains seem
    Suspended high in air,
A mystic world of island rocks
    From some enchanted dream.
The noon chime breaks from distant clocks
    Faint o'er the hot lagoon,
The yellow sails hang lifelessly,
    The earth lies in a swoon ;
We hardly know if sky or sea
    Is round us where we float,
There seems no life in all the world
    But in our sable boat.

The very oar-weeds do not sway,

    The seagull's wings are furled,

And on the shallows still as they

    It floats beneath the spell.

In yonder ancient island pile

    Each window lights a cell;

A great red wall shuts in the isle

    And dips in the lagoon,

And blank and shadowless it stares

    Towards the burning noon.

Great God, a sudden shriek that scares

    The seagull to its wings!

A brutish shriek, but not of pain,

    That rings and rings and rings,

And once again, and yet again,

    And then the silence falls

    Lonely and weird and sad.—

A world of life in yonder walls,

    And all those men are mad!

TO F. M. C.

STRANGE is it not, old friend, that you who sit
Bowered in quiet, four garden walls your world,
With books and love and silence,—sails fast furled
And grounded keel that hardly now will quit
Its stormless haven,—you sit there and write
Of human passions, of the fateful fight,
Of all men suffer, dream and do,
Denounce the false and glorify the true !

While I the wanderer, I whose journey lies
In stormy passages of life and sound,
I with the world's throb ever beating round,
Here, in that very stress and storm of cries
Make songs of birds, weave lyric wreaths of flowers,
Recall the spring's joy and the moonlit hours,
And know that children's ways are more to me
Than all you write of and I have to see.

THE SONG'S SPELL.

WHERE did you learn that music ?—for it drew
  My dreaming back down autumn paths of years,
  Touched chords long silent, and forgotten tears,
Recalled dim valleys where dead violets grew,
Soothed me with twilight, as it were it knew
  The very secret of my heart, and sighed
  For sympathy, and when at last it died
It seemed as if my soul were singing too.

Where did you learn that music, to allure
  Thoughts long in silence and submission pent ?
Oh such was Blondel's at the dungeon doors,
  So rang the song of captive troubadour,
Echoed along the moonlit battlement
  On far-off legend-haunted shores.

TO A CHILD.

Nay, child, awhile go back to play,
  Be happy to be young !
The world grows wise before its day,
  Leaves half the songs unsung.

And bloomless are its garden trees,
  Round all the ways are set
Forget-me-nots of memories
  And pansies of regret.

The meadows where your daisies are
  Will yield more dear delight
Than watching for the wandering star
  We may but watch at night.

I would not clip your wilful wing,
  Nor cloud your morning sky,
Nor draw across your path of spring
  The shadow of a sigh.

For Time will bring the bloomless tree,
   The roseless garden plot,
And on the bed of memory
   The sad forget-me-not.

ASSISI.

AN INTRODUCTION.

Di quella costa là dov' ella frange
Più sua rattezza nacque al mondo un Sole. —PAR. XI.

THE gates are shut, for here in the mountain nest
They keep the old-world custom, and the ring
Of battled ramparts holds the little town
Safe in its stern embracing,—twilight walls
With windows staring at the April stars,
Grey fronts of hoary palaces upreared
Like ocean cliffs against the sky.—Deep down
A few lights twinkle in the shadowy vale
That broadens into darkness, and beyond
The misty hills, and still the hills beyond.
Near by a fountain splashes on and on,
Intensifying silence, now and then
Some hound bays on the mellow air, the bells
Ring the reluctant hours, but all things else
Slumber profoundly, and the ancient streets
Are dark and solemn as befits a shrine.

Lovely in light of morning, touched with peace
In the gold glow of noontide, loveliest still
In the moon-radiant sleep, this mountain land
Of all earth's lands speaks nearest to the heart,
Touches a chord of memory, and relinks
Time's broken sequence.

     Here once lived a man
Who took God's literal word in earnest, chose
The child's interpretation, and forsook,
While a fierce world about him warred and wailed,
The path of glory for the thorny way
Worn by the feet of one in Galilee
A thousand long forgetful years before.
Tread softly here, for here his feet were bruised,
Here he was mocked and gibed at, here he gave
His very body to redeem men's souls
In that rough age of symbol, till a light
Burned in this mountain fortress that still shines
Round his forsaken altar, and shall shine
When altars fall and litanies are dumb.

This was a man like you and I who went
With song and laughter down the vale of youth,
With keen delight in living, in no wise

Secured from passion or withheld from pride,

The earthly dream had lured him :—suddenly

He heard the voice speaks once to every man,

And hearing did not stifle it ; he saw

The visible contrast, the old woe of earth

That ever cries for righting, he conceived

There was another kingdom made for souls,

Where love not wisdom watches at the door,

That whoso enters, enters as a child,—

And lived out his ideal ; such white lives

God takes for mouthpiece here on earth, secure

His word shall pass untainted.   Therefore he

Who loved the whole life-throbbing earth so well,

With such quick sympathy the very birds

Endured his gentle presence, the wild things

Fled not his kindly greeting, flung aside

The lute of young romances and stripped off

The sword and helmet, girt about his youth

The sackcloth of repentance, and went forth

A homeless pilgrim to the heart of man.

And lovely now across the sundering years,

Touched with the glamour of earth's morning time,

It rings, the ancient story, how they went
His new disciples on their helpful ways
About these Umbrian valleys, and fulfilled
The literal record of the life of one
That had not anywhere to lay his head.

But ah, the cloister's dedicated cells
Are tenantless, and silent is the shrine.
The fortress towers moulder on their hills,
And pilgrims seek not his deserted fane :
The world is so much wiser ! Only when,
As now, the moon is on the land, then ghosts
Flit round these shadowy portals, and the night
Rolls back long tides of centuries. So I,—
Waking an old-time echo by the walls
That Giotto decked and Simone, long since
When priest and painter first went hand in hand,
And still the memory of saints was dear,—
I, standing in the shadow and looking down
To where the lowlier tower of St. Claire
Leans woman's wise to the high rock of his,—
The last and lonely pilgrim, made my vow
Some day to tell his story and enshrine
The " saintly brother " in an English song.

TO M. T.

OH DEEM ME NOT FORGETFUL!

Oh deem me not forgetful, though I love
  The sunny pastures and the land of vine,
And golden walls where in the niche above
  Some shadowy saint smiles through the broken
    shrine !

For when the angel of the evening star
  Looks down the track of sunset, and there fall
The twilight dreams, and through the hush afar
  Some church-bell rings good-will at eve to all,

Oft in the twilight of my dream I pass
  To a quiet spot in England where the trees
Seem giant shadows on the misted grass,
  And silence turns the key of memories ;

And there are times it makes me mad to see
  Those red lights twinkle, hear the horse's tread
Along the old familiar road, and be
  Where all the mirth and all the love are dead.

NORTH AND SOUTH.

How I remember one day of all
That Tuscan spring-tide's carnival !
How I remember one eve when we
Leaned over the edge of Fiésole,
While all the plain lay in opal mist
Low under the ridges of amethyst,
When the gates of heaven seemed open wide
As the sun went under the mountain's side,
And over the sky in a flood-wave rolled
The tide of the glory of molten gold.

Do you remember the chime that fell
From the tinkling roof of the cloister bell?
Do you remember the tales we told
Of the dwellers there in the days of old,
While the reapers climbed from the slopes below
With scythes that flashed in the after-glow,
With the laughing eyes and the hill-born grace,
And the tale of ages in their face ?

Do you remember how marble-white
The towers lay in the May moonlight,
How the first few fire-flies came and went,
And just to live was a deep content?
How warm and sweet was the evening air,
As if all the garden of spring grew there!
How we seemed to have reached to a joy at last
That was not in the morrow and not in the past,
And only a word might have held it fast!

We were hardly lovers, yet more than friends,
If one begins where the other ends:
And was it the dream, the time, the place,
Or was it the magic of your sweet face?
For I can remember your least word said,—
When the blood is young and the lips are red,
Oh why should the dead not bury their dead!

Here, leagues away, are the plains that roll
To the Baltic shore and the silent Pole;
Dark belts of forest shut in the day
Low under the dome of the autumn grey,
With a gleam of red on the rifting lines
Over the edge where day declines:

The leaves decay and the chestnuts fall,
The chill Norse shadow is over all !

And yet, and yet, were you only here,
I might not fret for the waning year,
Nor hunger so for the valley wide,
For the starry blue and the steep hill-side,
And the tower of Arno dim-descried.

Pomerania, '87.

TO FLORENCE.

For the unveiling of the new façade, May, 1887.

IMPROMPTU.

THE strife is dead, the ramparts' ring
Is a flowery path for feet of spring,
   The old gates never close,
And well the Lily City rests
Between the hills' divided crests
   Through which her Arno flows.

The strife is dead, the broad-flagged street
Recoils no more from armoured feet,
   The towers are all laid low,
For White and Black have long been one,
As sunset after setting sun,
   And friend was laid with foe.

A people's love returns to thee,
Who first of cities learned to be
   A nation and a name,

Who never bowed the head to fate,
And bore the harvest of thy great
   To gratitude and fame !

For Rome is like some mighty wraith
Reincarnate by a nation's faith,
   But Florence did not die !
She earned her peace in ample tears,
And rests upon the stormless years
   With passion long put by.

But still the spirit is not spent
That bade the Ghibelline relent
   To save her from her doom ;
The love that softened Dante's eye
For Farinata's agony,
   Fire-tortured in his tomb :

The spirit which in the day of need
Was greater than the merchant greed,
   And armed her for the fray,
When stern Ferruccio hacked and hewed
And died among his hero brood
   On Gavinana's day.

The spirit which decreed the shrine,
That old Arnolfo's dim design
   First planned for Florence free,
That Donatello decked and gemmed,
And Brunellescho diademmed,
   And Giotto, ah, but he!

He set the marble marvel high
Against the limpid Tuscan sky,
   The tower of all the towers,
Her glory and her sentinel
With chime and ave warding well
   Our Lady of the Flowers.

And now glad bells ring out to-day,
Ring far down Arno vale away,
   To the mountain citadels:
Let Prato's to Pistoia call,
And let Pistoia's battle-wall
   Re-echo with the bells!

For where the old ambition failed
The love of after years availed
   Worked with as prayerful hands,

And Florence has her shrine at last,
The shrine she purposed, unsurpassed
  In all the alien lands :

Fair delicate spiral shafts and rose
Of window tracing and repose
  Of saints in solemn row,
And wealth of jewels set in gold,
And fretted carvings manifold
  Of marble white as snow !

Oh, hero dead, from your happy isle
I think that you look back and smile
  The exile heart returns,
For never dead were held more dear,
And pilgrim nations reverence here
  Your cenotaphs and urns.

Her work of years is done to-day,
And watching in their long array
  Her mighty sons rejoice :
The last upon the scroll of Fate,
De Fabris, from the silent gate
  Leans back to hear her voice.

Dear city of the hills, well done!
Smile on beneath the fair May sun
   In calm and conscious pride,
The fairest city built of hands
In recollection's loveliest lands
   By silver Arno's side!

A nation's effort is their prayer,
And thine shall rise on this spring air
   Beyond the blue above,
Worthy of Florence, Florence free,
Worthy of Florence, Italy,
   And worthy all men's love.

Florence, 1887.

TO G. L. G.

Less often now the rolling years
  Will time our feet together,
And seldom now the old voice cheers
  The march of wintry weather.

But friendship knit in other days,
  When hope was first aspiring,
Will hardly quit the travelled ways
  For fancy's new desiring.

Hope beckoned round the world, dear lad,
  And light we followed after,
And knew the grave and loved the glad,
  And shared men's tears and laughter.

We set our young ideals high,
  And if the aim out-soared us,
Still not to trust was not to try,
  And something shall reward us :

And what we found too hard to reach,
  And what we failed in winning,
May wait us somewhere yet to teach
  The end is the beginning.

We made mistakes in youth, my lad,
  But they will not out-live us,
The worst we did was none so bad—
  The world may well forgive us !

Long be it ere we two depart !
  Time make our friendship mellow !
I never loved a truer heart,
  Nor wished a better fellow.

"BRUMA RECURRIT INERS."

THE clouds roll down the forest
  And almost meet the plain,
One snowy peak, the hoarest,
  O'er-tops the clouds again,
    The brooks are babbling louder,
    The stream is swelling prouder,
      For many days of rain.

The belfry in the village
  Rings with a muffled chime,
The rooks swoop o'er the tillage,
  You see it's autumn time ;
    All things are dead or dying,
    And thoughts are turned to sighing,
      And will not run in rhyme.

A MAZURKA OF CHOPIN.

PLAY on, play on, the low lights wane,
  So, softly, softly play !
For your fingers draw me away, away,
  And dreamland comes again.
Are you 'ware of little stars in a pale sky !
  Play on,—and say no word !—
There is scarce the breath of a midnight sigh ?
  Or a frond of the fern-wood stirred ;
Was there ever a night so magic still ?
    Only a low moon is peeping
    Through the sway of aspens sleeping,
And a ripple frets the rushes in the rill :
Are you 'ware of little feet upon the grass,
      Tripping, rushing,
      Hardly brushing
Any feather of the frailest as they pass,
Of a twinkle of infinite tiny feet,
  And the kissing of tiny kisses,—
Never was night so summer-sweet

Blessed of the moon as this is !
They are threading in endless mazes,
   Lifting the drowsy fold
Of the lids of the sleeping daisies
   For a look at the eyes of gold :
Gossamer robes of delicate weft
   Cling light on the moony air,
Rosy petals, a pardoned theft, .
   Are bound on the streaming hair;—
Now round and round in a linking chain,
Round and round and away again !
They are dancing to the ripple they are moving,
   Keeping time to the glinting of the star ;
There's a glowworm for the lantern of their loving,
   And wedding bells are ringing where the heather-
     flowers are.

Can you hear their little voices, you would hear
   If it were not for the ripple on the stream :
Still, for a moment,—now you hear,
Marvellous sweetly, clear and near,
   Under that silver beam,
Songs of a wonder-world, my dear,
   World of a wonder-dream.

THERE never were such radiant noons,
    Such roses, such fair weather,
Such nightingales, such mellow moons,
    As while we were together!

But now the suns are poor and pale,
    The cloudy twilight closes,
The mists have choked the nightingale,
    The blight has killed the roses.

SONG.

You were the only, only one,
  A long long while,
You were the spring, and all my sun
  Was in your smile!

You were the cloudless crescent moon
  In quiet skies,
The stars that clouded o'er so soon
  Were your two eyes.

Oh why so much and not the whole!
  Was mine the wrong?
You were the music and the soul
  Of all my song!

New suns may dawn for you, for me,
  Stars rise again,
But you have been what none can be,
  My spring refrain.

TO ARISTARCHUS.

DEAR critic with the many tongues, again
   I come for judgment with my book of rhymes;
And since, dear critic, you do oft complain
   This youth has graceful fancies and clear chimes,
But ever in some soft and southern strain
   He sets his key to soothe us, let him strive
Henceforth with sterner weapons; I would say,
   Dear critic, not ten talents, no, nor five
But one poor talent fell to me who play
For whoso listeth on what keys I may.

And for the self's song ?—well, I would reply
   That words so issuing to the world belong,
To tear in its ribald humour, and if I
   At times have written all myself in song,
I'll keep my own soul's secret, none shall buy
   My life-blood in the public place to test :

He knows who sings what songs are of the heart,

   How the highest notes touch silence ; for the rest,

I would not hawk my sorrows in the mart,

Nor sell my soul to win the crown of art.

And last, dear critic, what you most impugn,

   These scanty handfuls for a season's yield,—

May I not answer, still the year's at June,

   And other fruits have ripened in my field ?

But now and then the lute is set atune,

   And fancy beckons in the wandering time ;

And so, dear critic, let us part good friends,

   And as of old be patient with my rhyme.

Farewell, to other lands my journey wends,

But we may meet again before it ends.

II.

IN EXCELSIS.

A SONG OF EVOLUTION.

E

IN EXCELSIS.

" Das Einige, woran mir gelegen sein kann, is der Fortgang der
Vernunft und Sittlichkeit im Reiche der vernünftigen Wesen."
" Und hiermit geht die ewige Welt heller vor mir auf, und das
Grundgesetz ihrer Ordnung steht klar vor dem Auge meines Geistes."
—JOHANN GOTTLIEB FICHTE.

THOU hast passed the fatal border,

 Thine eyes are open wide,

And where is that new order

 Should be on the other side?

The light of old is darkened,

 And knowledge dwells with pain,

Now fain wouldst thou have hearkened

 And turned thee back again.

So many foes assail thee,—

 The sorrow of weak will,

The sorrow of friends that fail thee,

 The hurt of loving still,

The sorrow of idle speaking,

 The sorrow of waning youth,

The sorrow of fruitless seeking,
  The bitterness of Truth.
Thou askest, who will show thee
  The thing that thou shouldst do,
And a hollow deep below thee
  Returns thine answer, who !
The devious ways are doubled,
  Thou hast doubted what is sin,
Thou art tired and dark and troubled,
  And disconsolate within.

Lonely soul, I know thy trial, thy denial once was
    bitterness to me,
      No white ray of hope hath found thee,
      All grows dim and fleeting round thee,—
      Only forms of things external
      Shadowed o'er a dream diurnal,
Only what the self discerneth still returneth for its
    essence but to thee.
      Thou hast passed through wildering mazes,
      Thinking in and thinking in,
      Till the spirit reels and dazes
      And the moving sands begin.

Thou has peered behind the curtain,
And the clouds seem ever shifting,
And the ocean darkly drifting,
And there is no sure nor certain
In the shadow world thou knowest
Save the grave to which thou goest.

Now no more thy choice is free
Face what thou hast willed to see,
Set thy nerve to face the gloom,
Bold to wrestle with thy doom,
Clear away all tangent issues,
Memory's weft of phantom tissues,
Fling the dear child dream apart,
Hug the haggard truth to heart!
Either less than nothing worth
Fruitless pangs for bitter birth,
Aimless wanderings over earth,
Any dawn of any day
To the life whose goalless course is
But the sport of unknown forces
In a worse than wanton play;

Or there must be something other, oh, my brother, than
    our nothingness to find,
Something still besought for blessing though confessing
    we are lost and spirit-blind,
      Something dimly apprehended
      Not in thee begun or ended,
      Vainly questioned by thy " whence "
      Out of thine experience,
Something that in all our being though unseeing yet
    as surely we pursue,
Which thy will accepts unproving, ever moving, ever
    fruitful, therefore true.

      What is this which whispering saith
      All thy being is by faith,
      Only faith and nowise knowing
      Moves thy coming and thy going,
      Faith in power to perform,
      Faith that effort is not vain,
      Good that was will be again,
      Faith that peace will follow storm :
      Surely thou canst find evolving
      From begetting and dissolving,

Something ever growing, gaining,
Through the transient remaining,
Not alone that sea's unchanging ever-ranging monoton-
ing rhyme,
But on every tide's returning
Surely dawns to thy discerning,
Something of the waves upcasting
That confirms the everlasting
As a shore for ever forming through the storming of
the ocean drift of time.

In the tale of ages hoarded,
Witness is of this recorded,
Wrongs that were and passed away,
Night that was where now is day,
Human needs that struck in blindness
Answered back in human kindness,
Harvests reaped in latter years
Richer for long rain of tears ;
This across the dark sea's drifting marks the lifting of
the cloudy veil and far
As we cry our no surrender, dawns the splendour of
Hope's solitary star.

Ah, but Hope, I think thou sayest,
    Beams on havens, smiles to peace !
Where is Hope, oh, thou that prayest,
    When the whirlwinds find release,
When the blind force wakes to raven,
    And the shaken hills fall down,
And the ocean whelms the haven,
    And the puny prayers drown !

Thou hast deemed the sowing wasted
Where the harvest fell untasted !
Years of labour unrewarded
Love's surrenders unrecorded,
All the pains that none may tell
Spent to do one small thing well !
Then the sudden storm arises
Big with passionate reprises,
Sweeps away what lives have striven, dearly given in
    their sacrifice of joy,
    And the wave of life is stricken
    And the generations sicken,
Or the mountains burst asunder, or the thunder bellows
    earthward to destroy,

Silence drowns the human cries,
Mocked and vain the effort dies.

Oh, but Faith shall overthrow
Utmost evidence of woe,
Seeing nature knows no treason
To the evermore of reason,
Nothing dies though all things alter,
Only faith and courage falter.

All these shocks of desolation
Are but birth-pangs of creation,
Last convulsions of the forces
That ordained the stars their courses,
Witness of a work not ended, love-befriended since
the dawn of all began,
Thwarting forces that dissever,
God's denials of the never
Ere earth settle down for ever,
To the silence of completeness in its meetness for the
excellence of man :
Nature lives and life fulfils
Those old laws which laid the hills,

In her wildest-seeming mood
Still benevolent and good.
Through the ruin o'er the wrack
Gems of life come throbbing back ;
Not by earth shall cease to live
What was never earth's to give ;
Life more live shall be again,
After death and human pain
    Man's eternity remain.

Come with me and I will show thee, I who know thee,
    to the solitary place,
Where the morning-lighted road is haply God is
    speaking plain and face to face,
    Far beyond the wildering city
    And the discord of its cries,
    Where our impotence of pity
    Draws a blindness on our eyes,
Where is life for aye renewing all the ruin of the used
    and the outworn,
Where you feel the conscious essence in quiescence as
    the flower-buds are born ;
    Where the woodbird fearless launches

On the wing he trusts to bear,
Where the waving forest branches
Stir an ever limpid air,
Where the world's heart throbs its fountain
Through the rent of granite hill,
With the silence of the mountain
And the small voice crying still.

Too long our lives have lain at ease
When simple joys have ceased to please !
Consider all this singing mirth
The eternal miracle of earth,
Very death implying birth.
A while agone and all was grey,
A mist was wrapped about the day,
The broken trees were black and torn,
The sky all joyless and forlorn ;—
Then see how simply and how sure
The mother nature works her cure,
A sudden thrill, there runs a sign
Through all the intricate design,
A little sun, a little rain,
And all the glory is again !

No human logic shall destroy
The mighty balance here for joy !

Is the heart not beating stronger
By one dread that dooms no longer ?
Joy thou hast if thou wilt use it,
Hope if thou wilt not refuse it,
Clearer yet from yonder summit
Eyes shall see that overcome it.

Up and on then !   Higher, higher
Climb the upland of desire,
Till the valleys fade from wonder,
Like a blue sea rolling under,
And the lowlier echoes die
Near the silence of the sky !
Art thou dizzy at the steepness, and the deepness of
    the chasm under thee ?
At the light which strikes so purely, very surely, thou
    art dizzy to be free !
        Far beneath the mist shapes roll,
        Brows may face the glory fearless,

Eyes are open wide and tearless,
  And self-conscious is the soul.

Here where seldom since the world was
  Thought has travelled, feet have trod,
Nature with a wealth as lavish
  Thrusts her marvels through the sod ;
In the silence, on the mountains
  Man has ever sought for God !

Dimly under roll before thee
  All the ages of the earth,—
Forms that cast the shadow story
  Of creation and of birth :
Phantom shapes of first existence
  Looming hugely up through time,
Shadows cast down wastes of distance
  From the mist-light of the prime ;
Giant strife of forces heaving
  Through a half-created day ;
Life surviving, strength retrieving
  What the torrent tore away;
Stalks a gaunt and huge-limbed nation
  Hunger haunted, born to dearth,

Compassed round with desolation
  Through bare hollows of the earth ;
Wandering races sternly striving
  With the infinite to do ;
And the good of them surviving
  For assertion of the true ;
Slowly mounting up from chaos
  Warring each upon his kind,
To the first prayer,—" Lest they slay us,"
  From a spirit born but blind :
Till the need of kindred uses
  Shed a fitful light on life,
And they swore their savage truces
  To the demon of their strife :
Then a little love like leaven
  Working upward, dimly seen,
Till beneath the sun in heaven
  Tracts of barren earth grew green :
And there rose the prophet speaker
  Pent in narrow grooves of race,
Here and there an earnest seeker
  In his own appointed place :
Sagas of the wandering nations,

Idol carvers of the lake,
Runes inscribed in mountain stations
Which the haunting spirit spake ;
Truth begets her own recorder,
In the drift and waste impearled,
Slowly grew the dawn of order
On the dark and waiting world.
Slowly light on light ensued,
Voices filled the Solitude.

Light on light ! for ever breaking with the waking to
the consciousness of mind,
But the love that needs must guide it not beside it yet,
long lingering behind :
Reason working blind and crudely,
With the passion of the child,
Strength and passion blending rudely
For the taming of the wild ;
While some Titan marked his border, welding order,
and on many a sanguine plain
Fell the corn before the mowers that new sowers
might replant the world again.
Rose the hero's intercession

'Twixt the human and his doom,
Heralding a new progression
From a darker deep of gloom ;
Till the forms grow plainer nearer
Memory known and dreamed and dearer
All that human effort made for,
Warred for, lived for, died for, prayed for,
Prayed in all the names that slumber without number
in the aves of the dead,
Balder Ormuzd and Osiris
Mark the height where man's desire is,
And the temples on the mountains and the fountains
and the oracles of dread ;
These and tides of Empire rolling for controlling
savage hearts and wanton hands
Till the wildest learned submission and tradition found
the law that binds the lands.

Fair creations pass before thee,
Sunrise crowned and silver shod,
Lit with all the halo glory
Of man's morning dreams of God ;
Rose in Greece the star of beauty

And the fables gathered form,
Rome proclaimed the star of duty,
And the stars outlive the storm ;
Slowly, spite the world's derision,
Through the old pathetic strife,
Gained and grew the stedfast vision
Of the seers who taught us life ;
How they stand out grand and stoic more heroic than
the heroes they dethroned,
Drank their hemlock mute and smiling, unreviling,
disregarded and disowned !

Though the forms obscured in distance
Rises one with mild insistance,
O'er the hero's incompleteness
O'er the code and o'er the creed,
With a voice of passing sweetness
Toned to touch the human need :
One among loud wildering cries
Still, with pity in his eyes,
One despised and thereby purest
One in bonds and thereby surest,—
Man's defiance round him hurled,

F

Standing lone against the world ;

And a sound like music thrilleth

Yonder dark and misty vales,

For a gentle answer stilleth

All the world of human wails,

Love is first ! on love relying,

Love the gain and life the loss,

Crowned with sorrow, stabbed and dying

On the shoulders of the cross !

Love is first, though all agree not,

Points the way, though all men see not ;

Though the road seem only steeper, depths the deeper,

for the height we have to climb,

Though mirages false bedizen our horizon, and a halo

decks the prime,

Though the aging eyes regretful

Search the vanished vales of youth,

And a memory half-forgetful

Gilds the bitter lips of truth.

Heed not thou man's false divining in the shining of

thy true and stedfast star,

Mark not thou the marsh light's luring the obscuring
  of the winded clouds that mar,
    Heed not all the groves of error,
    And the phantom thrones of terror,
    All the shadows of the sun,
    All the infinite undone!
    What is all the wrinkled past
    By the while the world shall last!
    These endure their little season,
      But the timeless eyes of Faith
    See the transience of treason
      And the impotence of death.
    Life shall pass and be reborn,
    Night as ever yield to morn,
    As surely as there dwells in thee
    The instinct of eternity;
    While through the changing chances,
      And by the conquered throes,
    The scope of life advances,
      The individual grows!
    Unbound by superstition,
      From forms and precepts free,
    His warrant in tradition,
      His law in Liberty!

Say through chaos dawned a True,
An Order, and a work to do :
And clearer as each deed is dared
The higher heights beyond are bared :
Say 'twas sorrow and 'twas sin
Human hearts were tempered in ;
War was but that peace ensue,
Falsehood to assure the true,
Lust for life to weary of,
Hatred to constrain to love ;
Death is but the trance that brings
Promise to the worm of wings !

Much is needed to surrender
Much of brave and dear and tender,
False renowns that once were true
While their work was yet to do,
Liens of nation, ties of lands,
Severed hearts and parted hands,
All of chaos that survives
Thwarting our unmoulded lives,
All the idols time has shed
Reverence over from the dead,

Much beloved of yesterday,
Worlds to do yet lie before us
Swell the mighty triumph-chorus;
Nothing good has passed away !
Look not back with longing eyes,
On before the gold age lies !

By those heights we dare to dare,
By the greatness of our prayer,
Ever growing, loftier reaching
To a royaller beseeching,
By the olden woes washed painless, white and stainless
in the tears of bitter price,
By the strength of our assurance to endurance of the
need of sacrifice,
Not by dreaming but by using,
Not by claiming but refusing,
There shall dawn on eyes unsealing the revealing of a
self that knows and grows,
And the stream of thy devotion find the ocean where
its meaning overflows.

So take the thread that seemed so frail,
Have faith to hope and never quail,

For all the weary woes of earth

And all the hollowness of mirth,

Accept but this divine in man

Believe I ought to means I can,

And comprehend the perfect plan.

~~Lift thee o'er thy "here" and "now,"~~

~~Look beyond thine "I" and "thou,"~~

~~Every effort points the next,~~

~~And the way grows unperplexed~~

~~To wider ranges, larger scope,~~

~~All things possible to hope !~~

Thou shalt

~~Till thou~~ feel the breath of morning shadow scorning,

and on spirit wings unfurled

Win the way to realms of wonder,

Rolling starward with the thunder,

Flashing earthwards with the lightning to the brighten-

ing the dark edges of the world,

Till the vastness shall absorb thee,

And the light of lights enorb thee,

And the wings on which thou soarest

Thou wilt need to shade thine eyes,

For the radiance thou adorest,

For the nearness of sunrise ;
Then thy strongest strength shall be
In thine own humility,
Wrapt into the holiest holy
  In thy worship vastly aisled,
Bend the knee and whisper lowly
  " Our Father " with the child !

TRANSLATIONS FROM HEINE.

Faint echoes of a voice that sung
    The song of every day,
With music on the bitter tongue
    That took the sting away:
For sweeter singer never smote
    On such a simple lyre,
Nor stayed on such a tender note
    The fugitive desire.
The voice is hushed that battled long
    With passion and with pain,
But from the fount of living song
    The echoes rise again.

I.

WHEN two that love are parted,
   With rainy eyes they stand,
With endless sighs and sobbings,
   And hold each other's hand,

We did not weep at parting,
   And no one heard us sigh,
But the sighing and the weeping
   We learned them bye and bye.

II.

About those little cheeks of yours
    Is all the summer's glow,
But in your heart, your little heart,
    The winter and the snow.

Some day, my well beloved,
    You'll know the counterpart,
When on your cheek is winter
    And summer in your heart.

III.

My eyes were blind in darkness,
　My leaden lips were dumb,
For I was dead and buried,
　And brain and heart were numb :

How long it was I cannot tell
　That I had lain asleep,
When there came a sound like knocking
　Where I was buried deep.

" Oh, wont you rise, beloved,
　Eternal day breaks fast,
And all the dead are rising,
　Eternal peace at last ! "

" I cannot rise, my darling,
 I cannot see the day,
These eyes of mine, with weeping,
 Have long been washed away."

" Then I will kiss, beloved,
 Will kiss away the night,
And you shall gaze on angels,
 And see the holy light."

" I cannot rise, my darling,
 The blood is streaming red
Where once my heart was wounded
 By a cruel word you said : "

" Then I will lay, beloved,
 To take away the pain,
My hand across it gently—
 It will not bleed again."

" I cannot rise, my darling,
 My brows are bleeding too,

I shot a bullet through them
  When I was robbed of you : "

" Then with my hair, beloved,
  I'll stay the wound it made,
And press the bleeding backward,
  And heal the wounded head."

And how could I resist it,
  So sweet and soft a prayer!
I tried to rise in answer,
  And go to meet her there.

Then all the wounds reopened,
  And wildly welling broke
The stream from heart and forehead,—
  And so it was I woke !

IV.

I murmur not, no, though the heart should break,
I will not murmur, lost love, for thy sake ·
The gems about thy throat may glitter bright,
But in thy heart is everlasting night :

I've known that long, long since I dreamed to see
The night that darkens where thy heart should be,
And knew the snakes that feed upon thy heart,
And knew, my love, the wretched thing thou art.

V.

We sat, sweetheart, together,
  We two in a little boat,
The night was still and the water wide
  Whereon we lay afloat.

The beautiful spirit island
  Lay misty under the moon,
We were 'ware of the ghostly dances,
  The lilt of a fairy tune.

The song grew fair and fairer,
  The dance swayed merrily,
But we were borne disconsolate
  Away to the shoreless sea.

VI.

The autumn wind 's in the tree-tops,
  The night strikes damp and cold,
As I ride through the lonely forest
  With my dark cloak round me rolled :

And ever with even paces
  My thoughts ride on before,
And merry of heart they lead me
  The way to my loved one's door :

The watch-dogs bay and the henchmen
  Come forth in the torches' flare,
And my spurs clank loud behind me
  As I rush to the turret stair ;

In her own brocaded chamber,
  Its scented and warm and light,

And that's where my love is waiting,
And I fly to her arms to-night :—

The wind in the dead leaf rustles,
And the oak-tree seems to say
Whither away—mad horseman !
Mad dreamer, whither away !

VII.

All night I see you in my dream,
  And you look so kind and sweet,
With a sudden cry I arise and seem
  To fall at your dear feet ;

And you gaze at me so ruefully
  As you shake your golden curls,
And stealing through your eyes I see
  The little rain of pearls.

You whisper a word in an undertone,
  You give me a wreath of rue,—
And when I awake the dream is gone,
  And the word you whispered too.

VIII.

You love me not—well, be it so,
  That seems a little thing, dear,
I look into your eyes and grow
  As happy as a king, dear.

You hate me ; has it come to this ?
  Your little red lips say so,
Well, only give them me to kiss,
  And take the sting away so.

IX.

They've fretted me, they've angered me,
  They've plagued me early and late,
The one of them with loving
  And the other one with hate.

They've filled my cup with poison,
  Embittered the bread I ate,
The one of them with loving
  And the other one with hate.

But she that of all others
  My bane and sorrow proved,
Was one that never hated,
  Was one that never loved.

X.

My story of love is written
  In darkness and in light,
Like a weird unhappy legend
  That 's told on a summer night.

"Two lovers alone and silent
  In the magic garden's walls,
The nightingales are singing,
  The moonlight's flicker falls,

"She stands still like a statue,
  Her knight is at her knee,
A giant comes from the wilderness,
  And the maiden turns to flee,

"Her knight falls bleeding on the ground,
  The giant stalks away."——
Its only left to bury me,
  And there's no more to say.

XI.

The world is dull, the world is blind,
  More tasteless every day,
It gives you no good name, my child,
  And has a deal to say.

The world is dull, the world is blind,
  And must judge you amiss,
The world has never known the fire,
  The sweetness of your kiss.

XII.

From my tears that have fallen a flower
  Is springing along the vale,
And the sighs I have sighed endower
  The song of a nightingale ;

And child, if you'll be my lover,
  The flowers shall all be yours,
And the bird with its song shall hover
  For ever about your doors.

‘

FROM THE "HEIMKEHR."

I.

My heart, my heart is heavy,
 Though May is the merry time,
I stand on the ancient rampart,
 And lean against the lime ;

Blue glide the waters under,
 Around the quiet moat,
A boy below is fishing
 As he whistles in his boat.

On the further side in miniature
 Is a friendly merry scene,
Of gardening folk and summer-house,
 And cattle and wood and green :

The women bleaching linen
  Trip down the meadow way,
In the distance hums the mill-wheel,
  And scatters diamond spray :

A sentry-box is standing
  By the grey old city-door,
And the sentry-lad red-coated
  Goes up and down before :

He plays with his piece and it flashes
  As he turns in the sunset red,
Presenting arms and shouldering,—
  I wish he would shoot me dead.

II.

The sea lay gleaming miles before,
　　The after-glory shone,
We sat by the fisher's lonely door,
　　Sat silent,—we alone.

The white mist rose, the flood tide grew,
　　The sea-mew circled near,
And in the eyes love watched me through
　　There gathered tear on tear :

They fell on one white hand of thine,
　　And, kneeling at thy side,
I took the white hand into mine
　　And drank them till they dried :

Since then I burn unceasingly,
　　My life is torn with fears,
You see the witch has poisoned me,
　　Has poisoned me with tears.

III.

In the old stage-coach together,
　All night till the dawn of day,
We heart to heart pressed closely,
　Laughed loud and chattered gay.

But as it drew to morning
　We had a strange surprise,—
A passenger between us
　Rode Love with the blinded eyes.

IV.

On the far-away horizon
　That the even-twilight shrouds,
Is traced the town of towers
　Like a picture in the clouds.

A damp wind blows and ruffles
　The track of the waters wan,
With a dreary stroke and a measured
　My boatman rows me on.

And the sun in its splendour pauses
　As it sets to light the shore,
Where all on earth I cared for
　Was lost for evermore.

V.

We sat by the fisherman's cottage
  With the sea before our eyes,
While the mists of even gathered
  And mounted up the skies.

Then one by one in the lighthouse tower
  The lamps were set alight,
And far away in the distance
  Was yet one sail in sight.

And we talked of storm and shipwreck,
  And the mariner's life, who steers
Between the heaven and ocean,
  Between delights and fears.

We talked of the North and Southlands,
  Of countries far away,
What curious folk dwell in them,
  What curious ways have they.

Of the perfumed air of the Ganges,
   And the light on its giant trees,
And the lotos cups, and the still fair folk
   Who bow to them on their knees :

How the Laps were a dirty people,
   Thick-lipped and short and low-crowned ;
How they roast their fish, and they chatter,
   And crouch by their fire on the ground.

The girls were listening eager,
   Then no one spoke at last,—
We could see the sail no longer,
   The darkness fell so fast.

VI.

Child, it would be thine undoing,
   And myself will surely see
That thy heart recur not ever
   To the love it bore for me.

Only to succeed so surely
   Reawakes a half regret,
Only thoughts will rise unbidden
   Did she only love me yet !

VII.

I walk the old familiar way
   The streets I know so well :
I stand before my darling's house
   Where none is now to dwell.

Too straight and close these streets are grown,
   The plaster has no stay,
The roofs fall in upon my head !
   I make what haste I may.

VIII.

They had loved for long, but neither
  Would whisper a word thereof :
They looked at each other as strangers,
  And thought they would die of love.

They were parted at last, and only
  At times in a dream they met :—
They had both been dead for ages,
  And hardly knew it yet.

IX.

God is he who loves the first time
Unrequited though it be ;
But who loves without returning
Ever after,—fool is he !

Yet again and unrequited
Loving, such a fool am I,
Sun and moon and stars are laughing,
And I laugh with them—and die.

X.

I am heavy at heart and wistfully
   I think of the olden days,
The world was once so liveable,
   Folk went such quiet ways.

Now everything seems hurried on,
   Continual urge and flow,
And God is dead up there in heaven,
. The devil dead below.

And all things wear a sullen hue
   Perplexed and old and cold,
And were it not for a little love
   There were nothing firm to hold.

XI.

Heart of mine, thou art not breaking !
   Courage, heart, and bear thy pain !
What the winter time is taking
   Surely spring shall give again.

See how much remaineth over !
   How the world is lovely still !
And my heart may turn as lover
   Where and whensoe'er it will.

MISCELLANEOUS.

I.

Lay your hand where my heart is, sweet,
In the little chamber, and feel it beat :
There's a carpenter grim is at work within,
Making a coffin to bury me in.

He is hammering there by night, by day—
It is long he has driven my sleep away ;
Oh, master Carpenter, finish it fast,
And let me get to sleep at last !

II.

The scenes come back to memory
   That faded long ago ;
Why has your voice an echo
   That wins upon me so?

Oh do not say you love me :—
   I know the best on earth
That love and spring are fleeting,
   And turn to nothing worth :

Oh do not say you love me :—
   Kiss on with no word said,
And smile when I to-morrow
   Bring back these roses dead !

III.

It was an ancient monarch
  —Dull heart and hoary head—
And the crazed old king had chosen
  A fair young wife to wed :

It was a gay esquire
  —Fair haired of merry mien—
Who bore her train of satin
  Behind the maiden queen :

You know the olden story,
  So sweet and sad to tell ?
—They both were doomed to perish
  Because they loved too well !

IV.

.

The small blue eyes of springtide
  Come peering from beneath,
They are the little violets
  I choose to make a wreath :

And musing while I pluck them
  Sad recollections throng,
And each of these the nightingale
  Interprets into song,

Sings out my dream so wildly
  The very echoes start,
And all the woods are 'ware of
  The secret of my heart.

V.

The letter which you sent me
    I read without affright,
You will not love me longer,
    And yet, you write and write;

Almost a little manuscript,
    And written close and neat;
If that were my dismissal
    Then why the second sheet?

VI.

Stars with little feet all golden
    Shyly pass and tread so light,
Lest they wake the earth that **slumbers**
    In the bosom of the night :

Each green leaf an ear that listens
    All the forests voiceless stand,
And the mountain like a dreamer
    Reaches forth a shadow-hand :

What was that across the stillness !
    Through my heart the echo rang ;
Did I hear my darling calling,
    Or a nightingale that sang ?

VII.

First I was near despairing,
   And I could not bear it,—now,
It's over, and I've borne it,
   But never ask me how!

VIII.

How the mirrored moonbeams quiver
    On the water's fall and rise!
Yet the moon, serene as ever,
    Wanders round the quiet skies.

Like the mirrored moonlight's fretting
    Are the dreams I have of you,
For my heart will beat, forgetting
    You are ever calm and true.

HENDERSON, RAIT, & SPALDING, PRINTERS, MARYLEBONE LANE, LONDON.

www.ingramcontent.com/pod-product-compliance
Lightning Source LLC
Chambersburg PA
CBHW030629270326
41927CB00007B/1369